HUNTER'S TIP BOOK

by Bob Marchand

Canadian Cataloguing in Publication Data

Marchand Bob, 1949-
Hunter's Tip Book

Includes index.
ISBN 0-9680571-0-1

1. Hunting -- Canada. 1. Title
SK151.M37 1996   799.2   C96-910164-3

ISBN 0-9680571-0-1 (Soft cover)

Published by: B.S. Publications
P.O. Box 2053
Kelowna, British Columbia
V1X4K5

Printed in Canada

Hunter's Tip Book

This is a book that will open the eyes of outdoor enthusiasts and woodsmen.

In it you will find pages of ideas that will enhance the abilities of anyone interested in the sport of hunting, or the simple enjoyment of wildlife habits.

The experiences of many people were used to compile the many fascinating and useful tips contained here.

By Bob Marchand

Acknowledgements

This book would not have been possible without the help of many people that I have known who helped me gained the knowledge for this book. My father for introducing us to the northern woods of Ontario. My brother Ron who helped me tremendously with experience gained from the trap lines, with his outfitters business and his knowledge of the woods. It was he who got me involved in flying bush planes and as a result ended up putting me from the co-pilot seat to the left side of the aircraft.

I would like to thank all of the trappers, guides, outfitters and bush pilots that I have met during my lifetime who have shared their tips with me. These people are to numerous to mention.
In particular, I wish to thank Christopher Lidstone, who came into town and had the computer which helped me put this book together. Without him this book would be sitting in Limbo. Thank you Chris.
And last but not least, my family, Sally, Chad, Joey and Terry. For all of the aggravation I caused them while I was engrossed in this book.

The Hunter's Tip Book is designed to make life a little easier for you. It's for the person who wants to learn tips fast and not read a book with stories just to gain a little information.

I hope that you enjoy this book and take it in the context that it was intended.

This book is dedicated to the memory of Ray Marchand
He was my father and mentor

About The Author

Bob Marchand has spent most of his life in the Northern Bush of Ontario in the small town of Kapuskasing. His family was raised on the benefits of wild game and moose meat.

Most of his time was spent exploring and learning the secrets that the woods had to offer.

When Bob was 23 years old he joined the City of Timmins Police Force. During this time he started a small bowhunting based business and as well became involved in outfitting.

He obtained his pilots license and logged many hours of float time on the northern lakes.

Bob was retired from the police force on a disability pension after a shooting incident and continued his love of the outdoors.

In 1993 he moved his family out west to British Columbia were he now resides.

Active in all outdoor interests, Bob was involved in many various organizations. He was a member of the Northern Ontario Tourist Outfitters Assoc, North Eastern Director of the Federation of Ontario Bowhunters, President and founder of The Timmins Bowhunters Inc, and The Kapuskasing Bowhunters. He was the owner / operator of Tri ouR Outfitters, and is a regular member of the Professional Bowhunters Society. He is also a qualified International Bowhunter Education Instructor.

Now in British Columbia, Bob is the secretary of the Traditional Bowhunters of British Columbia.

Bob has written many articles for various outdoor publications and newsletters, and many times goes under the pen name of "The Jungle Cat."

TABLE OF CONTENTS

MOOSE HUNTING TIPS

BLACK BEAR TIPS

BLACK BEAR INFO

WHITETAIL HUNTING TIPS

CAMPING TIPS

Moose Hunting Tips

Chapter One

Chapter One
Moose Hunting Tips

☐ Here's a good hunting tip that works well in areas such as Northern Ontario and North of the 49th parallel. In this area all waters flow north and the winds usually blow from the north. This hunting method is best if done from a canoe and is deadly when used by both rifle and bow hunters. There should be two people to try this method, a paddler in the rear and a shooter in the front. In your canoe, start paddling upstream against the current. As you are doing this, you will notice that the wind is against your back. Paddle for about ten to fifteen minutes, then call. If you get an answer, ignore it and continue to paddle upstream for another ten to fifteen minutes. Stop and call again waiting for a minute or two to see if you can hear anything, whether you do or not continue to paddle upstream for another ten to fifteen minutes. Continue this for about three hours or so. Now turn the canoe around and drift with the current. In this mode the wind is now blowing from the moose to you. As well the flow of the current in the river is now acting as your propulsion system and the paddler in the rear has nothing to do but steer the canoe in a quiet manner. Any moose which has heard the calling will probably be alongside the river looking for his "Love Cow". With the wind blowing from the moose to you and the river current silently taking you to him, you can literally float right up to them. As their eyesight is not very good they usually assume that you are a log, some debris or tree floating down the river system therefore you can get right up to them. The direction that the wind is blowing also helps to conceal any noise that you may make as well as eliminate any of your scent which the moose may pick up. You will be surprised at how close this system will take you.

☐ When calling moose, call down into the water. This method of calling will help the call to be clearer and as well will cause it to travel further. It will also help the moose to better pinpoint your position so that he can walk right up towards you.

☐ Did you only get a cow tag this year?
Many hunters seem to think that you cannot get a cow moose to respond and therefore just rely on luck to harvest their moose. Here's a tip that I know works and

that anyone can use very simply. When cow moose call, it is strictly an instinctive thing that they basically have no control over. To get a cow moose to expose her position simply walk through the bush with a wooden paddle over your shoulder purposely rubbing it along the trees as you walk along. This sound imitates that of a bull moose walking through the bush rubbing his horns as he is going along. This is done to signify to the cows that there is a breeding bull in the area and that he is making his presence known. This action causes a cow to instinctively call and therefore give her position away.

☐ The best moose hunting areas are those that have been cut over or in old fire areas. The new growth will supply an ample food source for all kinds of animals including moose.

☐ Making a bull moose think that you are another bull trying to take his cow can really get you results. If you cannot call moose,

..9..

try rubbing a branch, paddle or moose call on small trees or saplings to imitate that of an irate bull taking his frustrations out on them. Sometimes this is all it takes to get a bull to make that one fatal mistake.

☐ Many hunters think that a bull moose answers only by grunting to a cow's call. This is not true. A bull moose can answer in various ways. Many times the bull will indicate his presence to the cow or caller simply by breaking a small tree and a loud crack can be heard as the wood is broken. The rubbing of horns as he walks is another form of answering as well as low grunts. If you do hear any of these sounds you can be assured that there is a bull who has heard your call. One must also keep in mind that many times a bull will come in to the call silently so one must always be prepared.

☐ If you are thinking about what type of rifle to use in the harvesting of moose. The rifle calibers should go from 270 cal. up to 375 cal., with the common calibers being 308 and 30.06. If you are looking for a scope, consider what kind of country you will be hunting in. It is advisable to use a 3 to 9 power scope for open areas and long range shooting. If you are hunting in wooded areas and expect your shooting to be about 100 yards or less you should use a 4 to 5 power scope.

☐ Have you ever had an occasion where you called a bull in and couldn't get him to show himself, or come in any closer? If you are close to a body of water, try walking in it making sure that it is loud enough that the moose can hear you. The bull will assume that it is another moose and may just show himself. Don't worry he will know exactly where that body of water is. If you are calling moose on dry land, the same effect can be achieved simply by pouring water from a moose call or canteen onto the ground. Simply hold the water source about three or four feet above the ground and let her pour. The sound of water pouring on the ground will imitate that of a moose urinating and usually gets them excited enough to come in.

☐ Because your moose is such a large animal it usually takes a lot of time to take out. This can especially cause trouble if the animal was shot during the evening. Many hunters will gut their animals and leave it overnight in order to get to work on it first thing in the morning. The problem is that during the night the carcasses can be visited by wolves, bears, coyotes and varmints and they can sometimes leave little left for the hunter. To cure this problem leave a coat or some piece of your clothing on the downed animal and urinate around it. The human scent will usually keep the creatures away till you return in the morning.

☐ While scouting your area for moose there is something that you as a hunter should look for. Bull moose will paw the ground making a rut pit. They will then urinate in it, and perfume themselves by rolling in it. They do this to let the cows know that they are around and that they are ready to service them. These rut pits usually have a strong odor to them and if you find a fresh one you will know that this is a good area to concentrate your hunting in.

☐ The best times to go hunting are in the early mornings and evenings, although moose can be hunted during the day. On extremely windy days it is best to hunt them in heavily wooded areas as this is a more sheltered area. The moose have a tendency to move there under these conditions.

☐ Did you know that a moose can and will dive up to 27 feet under water to eat aquatic life? This type of food provides them with the calcium needed to promote their antler growth.

☐ If you are a bowhunter and wish to hunt moose it is best to use a bow that is at least 55 pounds in draw weight Try to keep your shots close, inside of the 30 yards limit, and forget about those far away "Hail Mary" shots. Razor sharp broadheads are a must.

☐ Many times you will see both sexes of moose on bush roads or in clearings and the chances are that they have probably seen you. What do you do? Try this! If you want to get closer for that good close up shot. Do not walk in a straight line towards them. If you do they will take it as a threat and high tail it out of there. The best thing to do is to walk in their direction but at an angle, taking your time. Walk in a zig-zag pattern as if browsing. In this way they often do not take you as a threat and you may be able to get closer to them for a higher percentage shot. As soon as you see the moose turn broadside to you, you can be assured that it's next move is to run. Now is the time to shoot and fast as they will not stay around there much longer .

☐ Do you want to be able to tell the difference in the sexes of the moose family? In the fall a calf moose stands about four feet at the shoulder and has a shorter nose than a cow. A cow stands from five to six feet at the shoulder. A big bull will stand at about six feet at the shoulder. The tracks of a calf will be about three inches in width. An adult cow's track will be about three and a half inches to four inches in width and a bull's tracks will be about five inches wide. You will notice that the bull tracks are more rounded at the tips than the calf or cow. It is believed that this is because the bulls paw the ground more often although this may not be the reason. Females, both cows and calves, can be identified by the white vulva patch which is located under the tail of the moose.

☐ Did you know that a bull moose will usually breed with only two or three cows a year? This is one of the reasons that the call is so successful during the rut.

☐ If you are hunting moose in warm weather, your chances are less than if you were to go moose hunting on cold, clear, crisp, windless days. The ideal time is during the full moon on the cold days during the rut. The animals will be moving around more offering you a higher percentage chance of harvesting your animal. When planning your hunt try to book your holidays using the phases of the moon and hope that the weather will co-operate. Rainy and windy days do not offer the prime times that we would like to see. Calling on cold days during the rut is the best time to get in a successful hunt.

☐ Ever wonder if you can use a scent to attract moose? Why not try this? Find a farmer who has cattle and have him notify you when he has a cow in heat. When the cow urinates, collect it in a container, preferably a big one, and take it on the hunt with you. if you find a game trail that is used by moose or even better a fresh rut pit. Pour a good amount of the urine on the ground and sit back and call. Even if the moose comes in during the night when you are gone the chances are good that he will stick around giving you an opportunity at harvesting your moose.

☐ If you wish to harvest a moose while hunting from a canoe, try cutting pipe insulation lengthways and place it on the sides of your canoe. In this manner the pipe insulation will silence your canoe as you lay the paddle across it or accidently bump it while you are attempting to shoot.

Bear Hunting Tips

Chapter Two

CHAPTER TWO
BLACK BEAR

☐ If you have seen a bear and wanted to get as close to it as possible for that perfect shot, consider this. Even though their eyesight is not the best their sense of smell and hearing is uncanny. Try to get downwind of them and as you approach try not to make too much noise. Keep in mind that a black bear is predominantly left handed and it will be the left hand that is doing most of the work, rooting stumps, turning logs, looking for food etc. With this in mind, try to stalk the bear from the downwind side and on its left side as it will be the left leg that will obstruct his vision more often.

☐ Have you ever tried to drag a water bed out of the bush? Dragging the carcass of a bear that you have harvested can really be strenuous and tiresome work. Why not take a small plastic tarp with you about four feet by eight feet and lay the bear on it. You will be surprised at how easily it will be to drag the animal out of the woods and your work load will be cut in half.

☐ Do you know how to tell if the bear that you wish to harvest will make book or not? Here is a simple way to determine the skull size of the animal that you are hunting. Take a styrofoam plate that has been used to contain meat from the local butcher store. Place it in an area that you wish to hunt in or near your bear bait (if baiting is allowed in your area). The bear will bite into the styrofoam plate and then spit it out usually

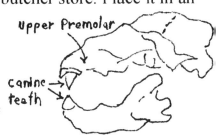

not breaking it. This will leave the imprint of it's canine teeth in the styrofoam. Measure the distance between the center of the two canine teeth puncture holes using the center of each puncture hole as a place to measure to and from. If the teeth are two inches or more you will have a bear that is Pope & Younge minimum which is an eighteen inch skull. If the teeth holes measure two and a half inches in width it will make a Boone & Crockett skull of at least twenty inches.

☐ If you wish to measure your skull to determine the size of it, do this. Cut the flesh off of the skull and either boil the meat off or let it bleach by itself in the sun.
If you wish to boil the meat off, place some bleach about two inches in a pail full of water and boil it placing the skull inside. When the meat is gone, remove the skull and allow a sixty day drying period. Take the top portion of

the skull with the lower jaw bone removed. Measure the distance between the widest section of the skull and the longest section. Add the two measurements and that is the score of your skull.

☐ Bear meat is excellent eating, however like pork it is subject to trichinosis contamination. Bear meat must be cooked to at least 147 degrees fahrenheit. There is no such thing as a medium or rare bear steak, only well done. If you want to keep the meat clean while dragging the carcass out of the bush just puncture some holes along the side of the body cavity keeping the dirt and debris out. Because a bear hide is dark, the meat and hide can spoil very quickly in the heat. Open the body cavity and skin out the animal as soon as possible. Try to cool down the meat by hanging it in the shade and if possible by a running stream in an effort to cool it down. Whatever you do, DO NOT place your bear hide or meat in a dark plastic bag.

☐ Many hunters look at bear meat with destain, you should however try making sausages out of the meat and you will find that it makes excellent table fare. Bear meat cooked well done over a bar b que and marinated in beer can really hit the spot.

Ever go spring bear hunting only to be eaten alive by black flies and mosquitoes? One or two weeks before bear hunting try taking one Vitamin B 1 Complex tablet a day and one a day while you are on your spring hunt. This vitamin will act as a repellent to the bugs as it will emit an odor from your skin which will keep them at bay. Instead of being bitten one thousand times you will only be bitten about ten. This drug can be purchased off of the shelf in any drug store or pharmacy without a prescription.

When you are hunting bear one must be careful not to shoot a sow with cubs. In most provinces and states it is illegal and rightfully so. It is best to watch the animal for awhile to insure that there are no cubs accompanying it. It has been said that it is impossible to tell the sex of a bear short of lifting a leg to have a look. This sort of activity is not looked upon kindly by the black bear and it would be best if you got this idea right out of your head. There is however a way that you can determine the sex of a bear and it usually is effective. Watch them for awhile and take notice of their traits while they are walking in your direction. You will notice that a boar will tend to walk bow legged with his front legs much the same as a muscle builder holds his arms when he walks. A sow's front legs will tend to be stiffer and straighter much like that of a fashion model in a fashion show. If you spend much time watching bears then watch for this trait. You will be surprised at how often you can tell the right sex.

☐ If bear baiting is legal in your province or state, here's how to do go about it. Enter an area that you know is inhabited with bears. Find a location to place your bait under a tree which offers cover from above to stop the birds from finding it. Also make sure that the spot that you pick offers you a good position to give you cover and to shoot from. Place the bait on the ground or place it in a 45 gallon drum which you have chained to a tree. Nailing a 45 gallon drum to the tree does not work as the bears can easily rip it off. If you do put it in a 45 gallon drum place heavy logs on top of the drum sealing in the bait. This will stop the varmints etc. from stealing the bait as only a strong animal like a bear can move those logs. If you are laying the bait on the ground ensure that it is placed in such a position that it offers good backing behind it and also a good shooting position for the hunter. Make a cribbing about three feet high and in the shape of a "V" with the bait inside the deepest part of the "V". Ensure that the widest part of the "V" is facing the hunters position. This will force the bear to enter the "V" shaped cribbing head first and in doing so will take the bears attention away from the hunter and also allow the hunter to get that good humane quartering away shot.. Start the bait with about a five gallon pail of meat scraps and cover it with the heavy logs in a manner to seal in the bait so that it will not be stolen by the varmints. As the bait is hit you can continue baiting with a five gallon pail of meat or you can cut back on the amount if you so desire.

Spread some stale bread and baking products in an open area visible to the crows and ravens near the bait site. Once these birds find this little gift these noisy birds will usually let every animal in the area know that there is free food there and this ruckus will bring the bears in faster to your bait area. Many outfitters often refer to this action as the bears dinner bell. Once they are attracted by the birds cawing it is just a matter of time before the bears will locate your bait pile.

☐ Another method of getting the bears to come in faster to your baits is a honey burn. This is done by taking a tall can and filling it about one quarter full of honey. Place it on a compact stove and heat it with a propane heater or torch being careful not to burn the place down. The honey in the can will start to boil and a thick sweet smelling smoke will start to rise out of the can. Burn the honey down until there is nothing left. Take out the can and stove and leave the area. The scent will carry itself through the woods by way of air currents and will bring bears in from quite a ways away even up to several days later. Your bait will be hit in no time as these animals will follow that scent, no matter now faint, right to it's source. Many hunters will even go so far as to make honey burns while they are in their stands in the hopes that the scent will draw the bears into their bait while they are in the immediate area. When this happens it is no surprise to see a nice black bear coming right into the site drooling as he comes. When your baits have been hit you will be able to tell because the logs on your bait pile have been moved and some if not all of your bait will have been consumed. Replenish the bait pile with more meat remembering to cover the bait with logs before you leave.

Try to leave extra bones on your bait when you are starting the bait pile. This will attract more bears as it will cause the immediate area to be littered with bones acting as another method of attractant to the area. After awhile you should be looking for entrance and exit trails. Once the bears will be hitting your baits on a regular basis they will become more confident in the area giving you a bit of an edge.

☐ The most prime time for hunting this species over baits is in the evening, although they could hit the baits at anytime of the day. Many hunters can and do attach trail timers to their baits and on bear trails to determine at what time the bears are coming in. Many persons are surprised to learn that these animals are one of habit and will always come back around the same time. These animals can also be taught to be creatures of habit very easily and they can and will work their schedules around yours. It is for this reason that one should check your baits at the same time everyday. If you learn from the information on your trail timer that the bear is coming in at about 6:45 p.m., try to get into your stand area about two hours before or 4:45 p.m. so that your human scent will settle. You can pretty well be assured that when the bear comes in it will be about 6:45 p.m. If you want to find out just how big the bears are that are hitting your bait, try bringing a five gallon pail of fine sand to the location and spread it on the ground in front of the bait or on the trail. The bears will step in it giving you a good idea of it's size by way of the paw prints left behind.

☐ Many hunters have trouble getting bears to come into their baits and have them go where you want them to. Many times this is in an area that is more comfortable to the hunters than the bears and they tend to stay away from there. One way to get them to walk into this situation is to do this. Soak a rag in bacon grease, honey, anise oil, or anything that may appeal to the culinary desires of the bear. The combination of these do not change the effects at all as these scents really peak their interest and they will react to it anyway. Take a piece of rope or cord and tie it to the soaked rag. Then drag it on the ground through the bush in the direction that you wish the bear to go. Many outfitters will tie the rag behind their ATC and drag it on the ground for miles leading right to their bait locations. It is best to use this method in grass fields or hydro lines. Areas where fresh grass is sprouting is another good area as it supplies a good food source for the bears. Once a bear finds this scent trail it is just a matter of time before he follows it to it's source.

☐ Did you know that the black bear is one of the largest killers of calf moose?

..25..

BLACK BEAR INFO

A sow has her cubs every two years. If she is bred by more than one boar or male bear it is very possible for her cubs from the same litter to have separate fathers. If the sow is in a position that she does not have enough fat reserves in her body to put her through the hibernation period or if there is not enough food available to adequately bring her and her offspring through the winter, she can abort the sperm within her womb.

One of the main predators of a young bear cub believe it or not is the boar. These males will kill and eat the cubs if given the opportunity. The sows, however will usually protect their offspring to the death and for this reason the boars will leave them alone if she is with them. Unprotected bear cubs are fair game. The cubs will stay with their mother for a two year period. After this time the sow will chase them away from her area. The female cubs however, will be allowed by the female to share her territory.

When cubs are born, the sow usually does not know it, and the cubs just feed on the sows rich milk. While in hibernation

..26..

the black bear will actually shed its paws from their lack of use. This results in the bears having tender paws in the spring when they first venture out of their dens. With this in mind as hunters, when you see a bear out early in the season you can pretty well assume that the den is nearby and that it will still be around for a while longer as the pads toughen up.

In the fall, before hibernation the black bear will chew off the hair on it's stomach. The purpose of this is to plug up their digestive system so that they will not defecate in their dens during the hibernation period, thus they can keep their fat reserves for a longer period of time.

In the spring, contrary to what people say, a black bear does not come out of its den lean and hungry. Think of it. The bears stomach has shrunk from lack of use and in fact if it tries to eat anything it will vomit. The bears stomach like those of a starving man cannot take a full meal. It is for this reason that persons will often see a grayish like vomit in the grassland and on bush roads. The bears hibernation habits conform well with nature in that when the bear awakes and starts to venture out from its den, it will drink a lot of water and start to nibble on the young shoots of grass that are spouting up from the forests floor and in meadows. The purpose of this is to get the bears system working and also to get the hair balls out of its digestive system which have been plugging up the bear. Once this has happened, the bears are still not lean and hungry as we often hear. It is during this time that the fish usually start to run. This is the bears first step towards solid food and they will usually feast on these until the run is over. Now the bears are lean and hungry as their system has been placed back into circulation. This is the time when they are considered nuisances, they raid garbage cans, come into towns and damage gardens etc. This is the best time to go hunting for the black bear as he is moving around more in search of food. It is also the prime time to start baiting.

Bears can most commonly be found in wooded areas: however, food sources dictate where they will spend a lot of their time. Spawning areas, berry patches and animal carcasses usually have bears nearby. Black bears are unpredictable and because of this they must be treated with respect. When going through the bush, if you do not wish to have a bear encounter it is best to try and travel with the wind at your back giving the bear a chance to pick up your scent so that you cannot surprise it. Make noise as you go along, you can sing, talk loudly, place some bells on your back pack, carry an air horn, baby rattle or just simply a can with rocks in it.

If you have a bear encounter, move away very slowly and try not to let the animal know that you are afraid. They can sense fear.

Try talking to him slowly and calmly, this may also work. If the bear starts to follow you slowly retreat and leave something on the trail to distract him from you. Things like a coat, hat or pack sack. It is not advisable to leave food on the trail as he could interpret this to mean that you are a food source and by this time you will be in enough trouble. If the Black bear continues to come towards you, try jumping up and down and waving your hands trying to make yourself look bigger. Some people will even bring an umbrella in the woods with them and open it up in the bears direction to make them look bigger. Many times a bear will try to intimidate you by making false charges. If an attack is inevitable, it is best to play dead. Lay on the ground in the fetal position and place both of your hands behind your neck to protect it. Bend your knees to your stomach to protect your chest area. remain as still as possible. Either the bear will leave you alone or he will bat you around a bit. He may even claw or bite you. Whatever you do, do not scream or move a muscle as this will only get him more excited. A bear can and will tear flesh and crush bones and believe me it will hurt like hell. But if you want to live, do not move. After a while the bear will leave you alone. He may even cover you up with dirt and leaves. Stay in that position until you are sure that he is gone then wait another good ten to fifteen minutes. It is always a good idea to let people know where you are going for this reason. If you are camping and don't want bears in your camp it is best to keep your camp area clean. Do not camp on game trails and place your cooking tent at least fifty meters from your sleeping tent. Your garbage should be buried or stored at least one hundred meters from your main camp and your food supply should be stored in airtight containers. Many people will hang their food in a tree out of reach from the bears and away from camp. Don't forget. Black bears can climb trees and they do it very well.

Whitetail Hunting Tips

Chapter Three

CHAPTER THREE
WHITETAIL HUNTING TIPS

☐ Using the phases of the moon is one way to help the odds in making your hunting trip a success. You should try to use it to plan your trips and give you an extra edge. Using this information can help you get the most effective times off of work. When the moon is full the deer will be most active all day and night with the most activity being in the evenings from about 3:00 p.m. till sunset. When there is no moon and up to one quarter of a moon you will find that hunting is more productive in the mornings from just before sunrise to about 10.00 a.m.

☐ If you want to find out if the rut will land during the season date's that you wish to hunt, why not try this method. Check your calendar to see if the new moon will come prior to the peak traditional rut date. By this I mean, let's assume that the peak traditional rut date is 15 November. Now if the new moon is after the 15 November you can pretty well be assured that the peak rut date will be pushed back about two or more weeks. If the new moon comes before the traditional peak rut date then the rut should take place at it's regular time.   ..32..

☐ Wind can really have an effect on your deer hunting. When it is windy you will find that the deer do not move around very much. However, if the wind really kicks up and is blowing very strongly the deer will get very nervous as all kinds of scents are being blown around and the whitetails nose cannot pinpoint the source of the smells. Because of this nervousness they will be on the move more and ever alert, which will give the hunter an extra edge because they will be more apt to travel on trails in an effort to locate the source of some of these smells. With this in mind it can be very rewarding to hunt on very windy days.

☐ Want an easy way to drag your doe out of the woods? Here's how, take a doe's two front feet and tie them behind her head with a piece of cord. Now take a sturdy piece of wood about two feet long and place it between the two front legs which are tied and pull. You will notice that the deer will slide out easily and that the hooves will not catch on branches etc. The move will also allow the hair to slide easily in the direction that you are pulling making your work easier.

☐ Want to drive a whitetail buck out of his mind during the rut? Find a scrape that you know a whitetail buck has been working and that you wish to harvest. Find another scrape that has been worked over by another buck in an area that you do not wish to hunt in. Shovel the dirt from that scrape and place it in a scentless container. Return to the scrape that you wish to hunt and place the dirt on that scrape. The scent of another buck on this working scrape will cause the buck that you are hunting to return to the scrape more often to find the offending buck. This action will give you more hunting opportunities at your buck as it will increase it's activities at that location.

☐ In many provinces and states it is legal to bait deer. If this is the case in your area find a place to set up your stand near a well travelled deer trail so that they will have no trouble finding it. Find a group of trees within shooting distance of your stand and pile several logs and trees against them about three or four feet above the ground. This does not have to be thick as just a few trees laid down much like a corral is all it takes. Make this "corral" similar to the bears cribbing in the shape of a "V" Place the bait into the "V" as far as possible as this will force the deer to enter head first and also give you a good percentage quartering away shot. As well in this position you the hunter will be allowed more freedom of movement as the animal will be facing away from you.

The bait that the deer seem to enjoy most are apples, carrots, corn, sugar beets and potatoes. The baits should be checked regularly about once a week and laid down at least a month before hunting season starts. The deer will become more comfortable and relaxed in the area during this time and they will also bring more deer into the feeding location which will give you more opportunities to pick the animals that you wish to harvest. Sugar beets should be used as often as possible along with other vegetables as they tend to last longer and you will not have to replenish them as much. It also forces the deer to spend more time chewing the chunks off and the crunching noise that they make will help to cover any noise that you make as you are getting ready for that shot. Corn, apples, and carrots are a nice touch but be warned that the deer can really go through them.

☐ Over hunting and area or a treestand location can really hurt your chances. It is best to have three or four options or other places to go to give that area a breather. As a rule when hunting deer, if you have hunted your area for three or four days straight, move out to another stand location. If you really like the spot that you were hunting in you can return to it in about three to four days.

☐ When setting up a treestand consider putting up two of them, one on each side of the trail or scrape that you are hunting. The reason for this is to compensate for the wind direction. You should always try to place your stand downwind from the area that you anticipate the animal to be. Place your treestand in a well shaded and protected area from view, but also in a spot that will give you the maximum shooting position as well as a location that will allow you more movement with little chance of detection. It also helps to find a camouflage suit that will fit well with the type of surrounding that you are sitting in. Once in the tree stand you can determine your wind direction by either lighting a lighter and seeing which way the flame is blowing or you can get a small squirt bottle filled with baking soda and squirt it in the air. Wind feathers placed on your bow or rifle can also help you with the wind direction.

☐ As with most high strung animals, a deer can and will run a long way on adrenaline. With this in mind it is a good idea to keep your mouth shut and your movements to a minimum after making the shot. Hitting a deer and yelling with joy can easily add more to your workload. The deer will make every effort to leave the scene and

..36..

will not stop till it expires. Usually the animal will be found in the thickest, dirtiest cover it can find which in turn means that you will have more work to carry it out farther.

☐ THINGS THAT GIVE YOU AS A HUNTER AWAY: SHINE, SHAPE, SIZE, SOUND, SILHOUETTE, SCENT AND MOVEMENT

☐ Searching for the right spot to set up an ambush for a nice buck? Find a combination scrape and rub line that runs through a funnel. A rub is what the buck does to the tree when he rubs his antlers on them scraping off the bark. This action helps to take the velvet off of his horns and helps to strengthen his neck muscles in preparation for sparring during the rut. These rubs can usually be found in a line through the woods. A scrape is an area of pawed ground usually under an over hanging branch. The buck uses the breeding scrapes as an indication to other deer that he is in the territory and that he is looking for does to breed. Several bucks can work the same scrape. If you find a scrape line and a rub line in a funnelled area between a food source and a bedding area, you can be assured that your chances of harvesting a buck there will be good.

☐ Always try for quartering away or broadside shots. This will give you the highest percentage chance to humanely harvest your deer. Never consider frontal or rear end shots.

☐ When hunting and watching whitetails at a distance, watch their ears. As the whitetail is feeding or busy with other whitetail matters, you will notice that the ears are always moving around like radar to pick up the slightest sound out of place. Keep this in mind when you are trying to approach a whitetail. Try to make your movements when the deer is looking away from you and it's ears are forward. When his ears are in this position they will help to block his vision behind him giving you a bit of an edge in getting a little bit closer. Another thing with the ears that you should watch for is that just before they flee into the bush they will put their ears back as they do not want them to sting as they hit the branches.

☐ Preseason scouting can really pay off in big dividends! At least two or three weeks before the season starts so as not to be too disruptive to the deer herd during the hunt. Take a walk into the area that you wish to be hunting in.

Established deer trails, rubs and territorial scrapes can all be used to gather information as to whether the bucks are using these areas. Keep in mind that this is in the early part of the hunting season usually in September and that there are often times bachelor groups of deer still roaming around feeding as the rut has not started yet. If you find an area with all of these ingredients try to be downwind of this area in a location out of sight in the early morning and evening till dark. In this way you will be able to see what kind of animals you will be dealing with as well as get a good idea of which routes or trails that they will be taking to enter the fields and feeding areas. Remember that it will only take a couple of days into the hunting season for the deer to realize that the hunting season is on and for them to change their habits and be more secretive.

☐ Ever wonder how to get the buck into a shooting position that you want? Take an old fly fishing reel and make sure that there is a lot of fly line on the spool. Now place the fly reel and line into a scent free plastic baggie. Get some reputable doe in heat lure, which you can purchase at your local sporting goods store, and pour it on the line on the reel in the bag. Do not use products advertised as deer urine or doe lure. That is usually all that you are buying and does not appeal as much to a buck as a sex scent. Wear rubber gloves and rubber boots when handling this and placing it out as deer cannot smell rubber and therefore your scent will be less prominent.. Place the string from the reel along the ground, as you unravel it from the reel walk along in the location that you wish the buck to walk. Make sure that you cross several deer trails and if possible a scrape or rub line. Also make sure that it passes within easy shooting range of your stand area. Do not leave the reel on the ground but keep it in the plastic bag and take it out with you. Any buck who crosses this scent line will follow it with his nose to the ground. They will travel back and forth several times from one end of the line to the other trying to pick up the rest of the trail. This is all you need to get his attention away from his surroundings and actually put him where you want him to be. A word of warning on this one, do not leave the reel and line in the plastic bag for long periods of time as it will get moldy smelling and not be effective again. Air the reel and line out of the bag and rescent it again the following year.

☐ Using cover scent can be very productive but can also work against you if handled wrong. Case in point. Many hunters like to use a cover scent to conceal their body odor. However using a cedar cover scent in a wooded area where cedar trees do not exist simply does not work. It does not fit in, much the same as an apple cover scent or attractant scent would not fit in a location that does not have apple trees. You must keep in mind that your house is much the same as a deer's home. If you walk into your house and there is a strange smell or something is moved you will pick it up right away. Animals are the same way in their environment and this includes smells, broken branches, scuff marks on the ground or anything added or taken away. Try not to disrupt the regular flow of life and keep everything as untouched as possible.

Camping Tips

Chapter Four

CHAPTER FOUR
CAMPING TIPS

☐ Have you ever had to fly into a camping spot or load up your vehicle and were stuck for room? It seems that often times you have to give up some of your comforts like a foam mattress and you will end up sleeping on the cold hard ground. Try this little trick which is used by bush pilots and works very well. Roll up your foam mattress and place it in a plastic bag that has no holes in it. Close the top of the bag around the nozzle of your vacuum cleaner and turn it on, the vacuum created will suck the air out of the bag and the foam and as a result the mattress will shrink to about an eighth of it's size. It will still be light and easy to transport.

☐ If you are looking for a cheap yet effective way to water proof your leather boots, go into any hardware store and buy yourself a wax toilet seal gasket. Rub it into your leathers and then lightly heat the wax on the boots with a propane torch melting the substance into the leather. Let it cool and rub it in. The cost is hardly nothing and the seal will last a very long time.

☐ If you wish to have a hot meal ready for youself while driving to your campsite and you know that you won't really have time to set up camp and cook before it is time to settle in, Try this! Place a roast along with potatoes, carrots, onions etc into some tin foil and wrap it up allowing nothing to leak out. Place the meat on top of the engine near the manifold of your vehicle. Place it where it will not fall down while you are driving. After turning it over every hour or so, or every sixty miles when you arrive in camp you will find that your feast is well cooked and that the time was well spent.

☐ If you want to keep the flies away from your campsite, why not hang a fish about fifty feet from your camp onto a tree branch. Place a half full bucket of water under it and when the flies gorge themselves on the fish they will fall into the pail drowning themselves.

☐ If you are troubled with mice in your camp and do not have a mouse trap. Why not try this? Place a pail of water about half full on the ground in your camp. Now lay a stick on it balanced with the centre of the stick on the side of the pail. Make sure that one end of the stick is resting on the edge of a table or cooler wherever you are having your mouse problem. Place a small crust of bread at the other end of the stick which is sticking out over the centre of the pail. The mouse will walk on the stick to get the bread crust and the weight of the mouse will cause the stick and the mouse to fall into the pail drowning it.

☐ When setting up your camp one should check first to ensure that there are no dead trees or overhanging branches within striking distance of your camp site. A strong wind can easily cause a deadfall to land on you or your tent and could take the fun out of your trip.

☐ It is best not to eat bananas in the woods during fly season as it emits an odor which attracts mosquitoes and black flies.

☐ Dark clothes, especially wet ones will really attract bugs so ensure that your clothes are light coloured and dry.

☐ Cooking your meals and doing dishes can really be a pain. Here is a way that you can cook your meat or fish and still have a lot of spare time on your hands.. Take your fish or meat and clean it. Wrap the food up in wet newspaper making sure that it is well soaked. If you do not want to use paper, one can use tin foil wrapped around it several times. Now, dig a hole in the ground about a foot deep. Place the food in the hole and cover it with the dirt that you have taken out of the hole. Build a campfire on top of the fresh soil and leave it burning all day if you so desire. The heat from the fire will cook your meal and at the end of the day or even the next morning you can dig the food back up. Your meal will be well cooked and is a treat to eat.

☐ If you want the maximum light from your lantern try placing a mirror or a reflective surface behind the globe and you will find that the lantern will cast more light.

☐ If you are in the woods and are suffering from hypothermia, try boiling a cup of hot water and add a teaspoon of cayenne pepper. Drink it down and it will help to raise your body temperature. If you fear frostbite you can also sprinkle some of the pepper inside your socks. This will work.

☐ No matter how nice a place looks for a campsite, never set your tent up on a trail. Animals, like people, like to use established trails and it would be very easy to end up sharing your tent with a bear or a moose as they walk through it.

☐ If you are using a propane lantern or stove for light or to cook with, try this and save yourself a few dollars. Buy your propane cylinders from the hardware store. Those thinner long blue propane cylinders that construction workers use to solder with are much cheaper than those that come with the lantern in the sporting goods stores.

☐ After many days in the woods it is usually a good time for a good personal cleaning. If you do wish to clean yourself with a home made sauna make a small tee-pee frame out of poles and wrap a plastic tarp around it. Light a fire outside and get the fire well fueled. Place rocks in the fire and let them get good and hot. Remove the rocks with a shovel and place them in the middle of the tee-pee. Make sure that you put more rocks on the fire. Pour water on the rocks in the tee-pee. The steam should really pour out of there. Replace more rocks as you require more steam and heat.

☐ Don't it just tick you off when you have wet boots and feet. Take your boots and drain the water out of them. Now, heat up some rocks and place them in the boots and keep adding them till they are dry. It works pretty fast.

☐ If you want your maps to be protected by the elements why not try to spray a thin layer of varnish on it and you will see that it will last longer and be more protected.

☐ Want to be warned when an unwelcomed visitor or bear enters your campsite at night when you are sleeping. This is especially good in bear country. Take your fishing reel and extend the fishing line around the perimeter of the tent. Take the rod inside with you keeping the line taut. Place the brake action on the fishing reel and you can fall asleep. If anything trips the fishing line the braking action being activated on the reel should warn you that there is an intruder in the camp.

☐ When picking a location to set your tent in, be careful not to set it up in a depression in the ground. Usually this is a well grassed area that looks very comfortable. That is because the area has been well watered and then grass has no problem growing there. If you do set up your camp there and it does rain you may find yourself floating in the centre of a little pond.

SURVIVAL TIPS

Chapter Five

CHAPTER FIVE
SURVIVAL TIPS

☐ If you ever get lost in the winter time and are thirsty, you will burn a lot of your much needed energy by eating the snow and melting it in your mouth then if you melted the snow with a fire and drank it after it turns to water.

☐ If you are lost and starving look for crows or ravens that are circling a given area. The chances that there is a dead animal carcass around that area will be good and you can use it as a food supply. If the carcass is being worked over by a bear and it means your life or his, try approaching it and see if it will run off. If he does leave, start a fire near the carcass to keep him and the other predators away while you work on this food source. If the bear is a grizzly it is best to leave it alone. Chances are that you have enough trouble already.

☐ When lost in the bush there are several different ways to tell you which direction you are going in. The sun and the moon rise in the east and set in the west. The tips of pine and hemlock trees lean east and ant hills are usually found on the south side of objects

☐ When you are looking for food, besides looking for small game and such, don't forget to check out birds nests for eggs. They can supply you with extra nourishment .

☐ If you harvest an animal in the woods try to utilize as much of it as possible. As a rule most game animals are very lean and a person can very easily starve to death just by eating lean meat even though your stomach is full. Make every effort to eat as much fat as possible and this will give you more of an advantage.

☐ If wildlife is scarce then your next move is to go the route of the bear. Although this does not sound yummy it certainly will save your life if you are starving. Rooting through rotting logs and stumps can bring you big dividends in finding grubs, ants, worms, maggots and their eggs. To make them easier to swallow, try mixing them with other food sources such as berries, and water. Even though this sounds terrible think of this. The black bear puts on most of his weight for hibernation by eating this type of food. Why not you?

☐ Scurvy can be a real threat to the person who is lost in the woods. One cure for this of course is vitamin C tablets. Chances are of course that they are not available. Fresh meat and fish will help as well as wild berries. If you do get scurvy, here is one way to prevent and cure it. Kill a caribou and leave the stomach contents alone for three days, then open it. Take out the stomach contents which is called caribou moss and eat it as sauerkraut. The stomach contents can also be used when the caribou is first killed however it will not be as tasty.

□ A beavers tail can be placed alongside a fire to cook. The black skin will bubble and peel off. It is full of nutrients and fat which tastes similar to bacon. Often times you will find a beaver carcass around the edge of beaver ponds. These animals are sometimes killed by accident as they are logging and the tree falls on them pinning them there.

□ Fishing hooks can be made by bending a nail or a bobby pin and you can use your boot or shoe laces as line. Worms, maggots and grubs will make excellent bait. Another way is to sharpen a stick and place a barb on it to hold the fish as you use it for a spear.

□ To get fresh meat without a firearm, try this. Build a box shaped container using small branches and prop it up with a stick. Tie one end of a cord around the bottom of the stick and hide behind some cover holding the other end. Place the trap on a rabbit trail or place bait in it. When the small animal or bird comes under it simply pull the cord trapping the animal in the box.

Another method of obtaining fresh meat is to find a well used game trail. Dig a hole on the trail about three feet deep. Place sharpened sticks in the hole point end up and cover the hole with branches or leaves. Any animal which steps on the leaves will fall into the hole impaling itself on the sticks and you will have a fresh meat supply. As this is a dangerous situation, one must cover up the hole when you have finished in this area. Another idea is to mark the pit in some way so that humans will be informed of the trap location.

Setting a snare in front of a burrow of a rabbit, ground hog, prairie dog or ground squirrel will also bring meat to your table. Some people will set a fire at the entrance of some of these holes and put wet leaves or wood on it to make a lot of smoke and fan it in the hole. Any animals that are in the den will be driven into the waiting snares which should be set at the entrances of surrounding burrows.

☐ Any food which you wish to cook can be done so without the use of utensils, pots, pans etc. Both fish and meat can be cooked on a spit over any open fire. Another method is to clean the animal or fish and pack it in a clay like mud pack. Now dig a hole in the ground about a foot deep. Place the mud covered food pack in the hole and cover it back up with mud. Light a fire on top of it and let it burn for three or four hours, longer if you wish. The meat will cook itself inside the clay mud pack and when you take it out and remove the mud pack, all the feathers and skin will come off with it leaving you with nothing but well cooked meat.

☐ If you ever happen to be in a bush plane that crashes look for an Emergency Locator Transmitter or ELT. This little device is supposed to transmit upon impact with the ground the location of the downed aircraft. It comprises of a small metal box and is usually red in color.

The ELT is usually mounted in the rear of the aircraft, look for it and make sure that it is in the transmit mode. To see if it is working turn the aircraft radio on and put it on frequency 121.5 or 143. This is the emergency frequency and from it you should be able to pick up the signal from your ELT. If you do not hear it, check the ELT again and ensure that it is on. The ELT has its own source of battery power. This unit must be checked yearly according to federal regulations so you will know that the batteries are good. To continue longer operation in cold weather try to keep the battery warm and it will give the ELT longer operating life. Placing the ELT in your jacket will keep the battery warm and allow it to last longer. Stay with the aircraft, it is easier to find and from it you can obtain shelter and fuel for the fire from the fuel tanks (do not light a fire close to the aircraft). All aircraft are required by law to carry a first aid kit and many have survival kits as well. If wing covers are in the aircraft spread them on the ground as they will be easier to spot from the air. They also make warm blankets. Take off the front engine cowlings and turn them shiney side up to help catch the sun's rays and offer the chance of a reflecting image to be visible to searching aircraft. Remember to keep the snow off of the wings to offer higher visibility.

☐ Three of anything is considered to be a distress signal. Three shots and three signal fires being the most common. If you decide to light three signal fires it is best to have them already made up and ready to light. When you hear

..55..

an aircraft or suspect that help is near, light them readily.

To help the searchers find your location more easily have plenty of green boughs and wet wood to place on the fire. This will cause a thick smoke and will help them find you sooner. If you require a thick black smoke and you are near a downed aircraft, take the oil from the engine crankcase and keep it on hand for just 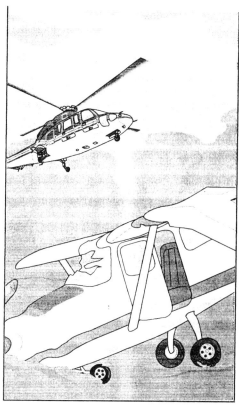 that purpose. If your aircraft had wheels or amphibious floats you can also burn the tires on them to obtain more black smoke. If there is a landing strip nearby the oil can be used to make a smudge pot to mark the location for the searching aircraft and it will also supply the landing aircraft with information as to which way the wind is blowing to assist them in landing.

☐ Mosquitoes and black flies can be so bad in some areas that they can kill a man in the bush. To help rectify this problem use smoke to keep them away. Standing in the smoke and saturating your clothes and body will help to repel the little critters. Another method to fly proof yourself is to cover the exposed skin  with mud. Putting strips of birch bark between your skin and the socks will prevent them from biting through the sock material.

☐ If you have been injured as a result of an accident and your wounds become infected you are in serious trouble. If there is no penicillin around and there is no other alternative, try eating moldy bread or cheese. This is the basic ingredient in penicillin and it could save your life.

☐ If you build a fire while lost, you should do it in a location which will give you the biggest benefit. If possible try to place it in a open spot that is close enough to your shelter to supply you with heat and warmth with little inconvenience on your part. Try to place it near a rock face or you can build a small wall made out of green logs. This wall or rock face will help reflect the heat towards your shelter for optimum performance. Do not build a fire under a tree as there is a real danger of it burning down as well as a chance that the melting snow will help to put your fire out.

☐ If you happen to be lost in an area that has an abundance of squirrels and wish to use them as a food source try this. Find a tree that has an indication that there is heavy squirrel activity. This is easily recognizable from the pile of shells from nuts and pine cones in that location.
Once you have found an area such as this, lean a tree about three inches in diameter against the tree that the shells are found in. Now tie small snares with light wire or shoe laces and tie the other end onto the leaning tree. The squirrels will use this log and get caught in the snares. If you have no snare wire and you are the victim of an aircraft crash you can obtain the wire from under the dash area of the plane. Chances are it will not be needed anymore anyway.

General Hunting Tips

Chapter Six

CHAPTER SIX
GENERAL HUNTING TIPS

☐ If you are transporting meat a long distance in a canoe, boat or truck it is best to keep the meat as cool as possible so that it will not spoil.
To do this, place branches about three inches wide on the bottom of the canoe and lay the two front quarters on top 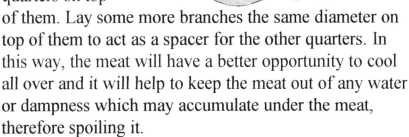 of them. Lay some more branches the same diameter on top of them to act as a spacer for the other quarters. In this way, the meat will have a better opportunity to cool all over and it will help to keep the meat out of any water or dampness which may accumulate under the meat, therefore spoiling it.

☐ There seems to be a misconception among many hunters that the animal they have just shot should have it's throat cut as soon as possible in order for it to bleed properly. The reasoning goes back to the days of the old time butcher shops when they slaughtered the animals. They would knock the animal unconscious and while the animals heart was still pumping they would cut it's throat and the pumping heart would bleed the animal out.

This action, in turn would allow the meat to be more tender and tastier as the blood was removed from the animal's system. There is no need to do this with an animal that has been shot and that is already dead. The heart is no longer pumping and for this reason cutting the throat does nothing but ruin a good neck roast and possibly damage the cape of the animal if you wish to have your head mounted.

☐ When hanging the quarters of your downed game in the woods to cool down, try hanging it on a meat pole that is placed in a well shaded area away from sunlight. If possible, try hanging it next to a running creek or river as the temperature near a water source is considerably cooler. Wrap the meat in a cheese cloth to keep off the dirt and flies. Check the meat several times during the day to ensure that there are no flies laying eggs on it and to see that the meat is cooling down properly. Many people will cover the meat with pepper in an effort to keep the flies from it. Do not wrap your meat or hide in plastic bags.

☐ Want to learn an old native trick for calling in deer and varmints? Take a blade of grass and place it between your two thumbs putting your hands together.

Make sure that the grass is taut. Blow into the blade of grass between your thumbs. The resulting noise imitates that of a shrill whistle which the animals will respond to.

☐ If you want to save yourself a few bucks while trying to keep your meat clean, here's how to go about it. Once the meat is down and hanging, cover the meat with cheese cloth. If you buy the cloth type meat bags in a sporting goods store you will pay more. Why not go to a grocery store and buy the same cheese cloth that is used as a cleaning rag? You will end up paying less and get the same job done.

☐ Many times both gun and bow hunters have gone in to sit on their treestands only to find out that someone has stolen them. To prevent this from happening, try locking the treestand with a length of chain to the tree. As an extra precaution one can remove the tree steps out of the tree when leaving. Remember, if you take the tree steps out try not to place them back again in the same holes, as they will become looser and more dangerous..

☐ If you are planning a hunting trip, try to make an extra effort and have the vehicle filled the night before or have someone fill it for you. The fumes from the gas and the possibility of overfill is one of the worst sources of scent which can give you away to the animal that you are hunting.

☐ If you are going to your hunting or camping spot and the roads are greasy and slippery, try letting some of the air out of your tires. The extra traction now will allow you to go that extra distance and not ruin your tires.

☐ Do you want a cheap method of eliminating your scent and body odor while hunting? Place your hunting clothes in a scent free plastic garbage bag along with several ounces of baking soda. It will absorb any odors that can give you away.

☐ Have you ever had an occasion when you had to drag your deer out of the woods and your rifle kept sliding off of your shoulder? Try sewing a button on the shoulder of your hunting coat with heavy thread. The sling will not slid off, the rifle is easily accessible and its presence will not interfere with you if you need your rifle in a hurry.

☐ Do you want an easy way to clean a grouse or partridge? Once the bird is down and as soon as possible afterwards before rigormortus sets in, place the bird on its back with the legs facing you and step on both wings. In this way the bird is facing breast up on the ground between both feet that are standing on the wings. Grab the birds feet in both hands and pull up. The legs, back and innards will all come out leaving behind only the wings and breast. The wings can then be easily broken off and removed.
Caution should be used here however, as in many provinces and states it is illegal to remove the wings from the birds while in transit from the woods to the residence. If you are stopped by conservation officers they may want to see one wing attached so that they can identify the species. The wing can be removed after you get home.

☐ If you want to remove the hide from any animal that you have just harvested, try taking it off as soon as possible. You will find that removing the skin as soon as the animal is down requires little effort. The longer the hide stays on, the harder it is to remove.

☐ If you are concerned about the scent of your clothing and want to save yourself a few dollars try this: wash your clothes in a washing machine that has already run through it's cycle with no soap. Then place the clothes in the washing machine and add baking soda. DO NOT USE SOAP. Take the hunting clothes out of the washer and hang them outside to dry. Placing them in a dryer can easily add extra odor to them from static cling materials and the like.

☐ If you are hunting mountain goats, an easy way to get an inquisitive billy to come to you is to place a white sheet over a sheep sized rock and find a hiding place nearby. Pretty soon the goat will walk up to it to check it out.

Bowhunting Tips

Chapter Seven

CHAPTER SEVEN
BOWHUNTING TIPS

☐ If bowhunting is your bag, then try this little tip while you are in the field; it could save you a lot of frustration and even save your hunting trip.

It is very easy to accidentally cut your bow string with a razor sharp broadhead while you are on your hunt. Before going on the hunt take a spare bowstring and place it on your bow stretching it for a while. Set the nok point on the string and then remove it. Replace your old string, place the new string in a plastic tube and tape it to your quiver which is usually attached to your bow. It will always be there when you need it.

☐ As feathers are far more forgiving and faster than vanes, the problem seems to be keeping the feathers in shape. When you come home and your feathers are ratty looking, wet and disheveled, a simple method is to steam them back into shape. Take an old oil squirt can and fill it halfway with water. Put the can on the stove and bring it to a boil. The steam pressure produced from the nozzle will quickly revitalize your feathers.

☐ Have you ever shot at a deer only to have it jump the string? When setting up your treestand or shooting position near a deer trail or a scrape, try to have it within an eighteen yard radius from the target location or past thirty two yards. Because of the close distance within eighteen yards, the animals reaction time is not fast enough and after thirty two yards they usually will not hear it coming. This is one of the reasons why traditional bowhunters have a higher recovery rate. They realize the limitations of their weapons and usually only take close shots. Remember shots over forty yards should be discouraged.

☐ If you use razor type broadheads and harvest an animal, be careful. If you pull the arrow out of the animal, check the head to ensure that all of the razor heads are still on. If there is one missing, use caution as there is a good chance that the blade is still inside the animal. Be careful, there is a good chance that you can cut yourself. In your excitement of harvesting the animal and cleaning it, it would be fairly easy to accidentally cut yourself on the missing broadhead and not know it. Your blood would mix with that of the animal and because of its razor sharpness you would probably not realize that you were cut. Several bowhunters have already been killed because of this mistake. If a blade is not recovered somewhere in the meat, please do not forget to tell the butcher.

☐ When using fixed broadheads while you are hunting, you should have as much of a cutting edge as possible in order to humanely harvest your animal. Why don't you try this? Sharpen the back blades on your fixed heads. In this way you will have the maximum cutting edge that will do it's job effectively and efficiently cutting every muscle, vein, artery, nerve etc., that it comes in contact with. Remember that this type of head will also cut as it works its way inside and out.

☐ Thinking of using aerial photographs on your hunt? One of the most productive methods of scouting your hunting areas is to obtain aerial photographs of the region that you wish to hunt in. Study the lay of the land and you will be surprised at the funnel areas that seem to jump right out at you. Animals travel these funnel areas to make maximum use of the terrain and cover in getting from one area to another.

If you are using shooting gloves that are too loose and want them to fit more comfortably try this. Soak them in water, place them on your hand and let them dry there using a hair dryer to help dry them off. The leather will shrink and the shooting gloves will form a perfect fit to your hand.

While shooting at an animal with a bow and arrow, pick a spot. Do not aim at the whole animal. This is a common mistake that a lot of bowhunters make. Another mistake is that they are concentrating so much on picking a spot that they fail to check the path of an arrow. Make sure that branches and obstructions are not between you and your target. Meat tastes so much better than bark.

Ever have your broadheads start to rust on you after they have been exposed to dampness and rain? To prevent this from happening, after sharpening them, lightly coat them with Vaseline or oil. Besides preventing them from rusting it also helps keep them sharp longer.

☐ How many times have you been out hunting in the rain and come back with your fletching looking like a drowned bird? Buy some of those baby bottle liners at your local drug store. They cost almost nothing. Drop the fletch end of your arrow into the liner and punch the nock end through the bottom of it. They will stay on there while you are hunting and will keep your feathers nice and dry.

☐ If you are thinking of buying a new bow, consideration of how well you can handle that particular bow and the poundage is a must. The bow should not be considered just because of arrow speed. A sharp broadhead on a heavier arrow will do much more damage than a fast flat shooting bow with a light arrow. Want proof? Take two balls, a golf ball and a ping pong ball. Throw them as hard as you can into a snow bank. Which one will go in the furthest? Also take into consideration that a light fast, arrow is easier to deflect than a slow heavier one.

☐ If you are in the market for a good broadhead consider this. You should purchase a broadhead that starts cutting immediately on impact. By this, I mean a head whose blades start cutting from the point up. Broadheads whose points are conical or chisel shaped, lose a lot of their penetration and cutting ability as they have to puncture the hide first before they start to cut. To prove this theory try taking an old piece of leather and stretching it taut. Take two different heads, one with a conical or chisel point and one with a point on it that starts cutting right away. Mount

them both on arrows and push the heads down into the leather to see which head offers the least amount of resistance to penetrate the leather. Quite a difference eh!

☐ After making a hit on your animal, do not move or make a sound. The animal will run about thirty to forty yards and stop to see what the danger was. They often do not realize that they are hit because of the razor sharpness of the broadhead. They will tire quickly and lie down to rest where they will fall asleep from lack of oxygen in their blood stream and expire. Shouting and moving will give them cause to run on pure Adrenalin, this will give you a longer tracking job and more work.

☐ When tracking a wounded animal keep this in mind. Every animal including humans have about one ounce of blood for every pound of body weight. As an example, if a deer weighs 200 pounds then that animal has 200 ounces of blood in it's system. In order for that animal to collapse from blood loss he must lose 1/3 of his blood or 70 ounces. That is a lot of blood. Remember that an arrow kills by hemorrhaging. The animal dies from lack of oxygen in its blood stream and literally falls asleep on its feet. A large amount of blood will remain unseen as it will accumulate in the body cavity of the deer.

□ When approaching a downed animal, come at it from behind. Also, keep in mind that animals do not die with their eyes closed. If its eyes are closed then you have a wounded animal on your hands. Watch out and put another  arrow into him to finish it off. If you want to see if the animal is dead when it's eyes are open simply touch the eye with the tip of your arrow. Watch out for sharp hooves and horns.

□ Want to silence your bow for those close up shots? Cover the inside of the riser of your bow with Dr. Scholl's foot padding. It is cheaper than buying it from a dealer and the mole skin really cuts down on the noise if you should accidentally bump your arrow against the inside of your bow.

☐ Here are some tips for you treestand hunters. Pick your stand location with care, and try to find a route into the area where you can travel undetected. Using rubber boots is especially helpful as animals cannot smell rubber, it also helps to keep human odor at a minimum. The height that you should put your treestand up should be at least fourteen feet. If you go too high it could affect your shooting and the angle of arrow penetration could cause less than a fatal hit. You should always use a pull up rope when you are using your treestand. When shooting from an elevated position such as a hill top or treestand and you are using sights on your bow, remember that the arrow will strike a little higher than where you are aiming. With this in mind you should make a little effort to aim a tad lower. Remember that if a deer jumps the string it can drop a full body length in 1/10 of a second.

☐ When setting up your treestand keep this in mind, if your stand is in an area that is affected by wind. Thermal winds travel in an upwards direction in the morning and a downward direction in the evening.

☐ There are several different treestands to choose from and the choice is yours. Here is one thing to keep in mind. Climbing stands can be very dangerous and can cause you serious harm and injury. Here is an example and is something to think about while you are choosing a safe treestand. On some of the climbing type treestands the seat assemblies wrap around the tree at chest level. You also wrap the bottom platform around the tree at foot level putting your feet into the stirrups. You use the seat section to pull yourself up and raise the foot platform up with the stirrups. The process is repeated again and again until the required height is achieved. The problem is that sometimes the user will lose his grip on the seat section and fall backwards. This action causes the user to break his legs between the feet which are in the stirrups and the knees which are carrying the momentum of the body weight. The result is that you will hang there upside down until you are found, dead or alive. This is one very good reason as to why you should tell people where you are hunting.

Taxidermy
Tips

CHAPTER EIGHT

CHAPTER EIGHT
TAXIDERMY TIPS

☐ Want to know the correct method to preserve your bear hide? Here's how!

Handle your hide carefully. Dragging it on the ground causes the hide to bruise and creates hair slippage.

Gut and process the bear as soon as possible, as the day's heat can cause the hide and meat to spoil very fast. If the bear was shot in the stomach make sure to wash the stomach acid off of the face and body. This acid will continue to work even while the hide is frozen and is responsible for 75% of the reason that hair slippage occurs.

When skinning the hide, start at the palm of each foot to the center of the back.

Proceed along the stomach straight up to the beginning of the head as illustrated. Be sure to leave the head and paws attached to the hide, the taxidermist would be better off to remove them. Skin spring bears as close to the hide as possible, you will know that you have done a good job when you see a bluish, black color on it. Fall bears have a heavy coat on them, their guard hair roots are further inside the skin and if you are not careful you can cut off these roots if you cut too close to the hide. In doing this the hair can fall out of the hide ruining it.

☐ When storing the hide salt it well making sure to place it heavily around the bullet or arrow hole. Roll it up, fur side out, put it in a burlap bag, NOT PLASTIC, and freeze it as soon as possible. Do not fold the hide up with the head inside. When bringing it to the taxidermist, be sure to have your expired bear license with you as many taxidermists must register the animals taken into their shop.

☐ If you wish to have a head or shoulder mount of your bear, deer, moose, elk etc. Be sure to leave enough cape on the animal for the taxidermist to work with. Nothing looks worse than a head mount with no neck.

☐ When bringing birds in such as ducks, grouse, owls, etc. Try removing any blood that may be on the feathers by carefully wiping the wet fluid and blood off with a soft wet paper towel or damp cloth. Try not to ruffle the feathers while rolling up the bird in a newspaper. Keep the bird in a cool location and freeze it as soon as possible. Many birds such as owls, hawks, and eagles require special permits from your local conservation office. The taxidermists cannot legally work on them without this.

☐ When bringing in the head of a trophy it is best to skin out the cape and bring the head in with the skull and cape still attached. Let the taxidermist do the proper job of skinning the head out. Many times this is impossible, however because of the distance to carry it out and also because of the weight factors in transportation. If this is the case, cape out the head of the animal and cut the hide down the center of the back towards the head as shown. Then cut from the end of that cut in two different directions towards the antlers. Take your knife and carefully peel the skin back around the antlers exposing the skull. Skin out the rest of the head allowing deep cuts to be made in the meat around the ears being extra careful not to cut the hide. The taxidermist can remove the surplus meat in his own time. When you come to the lips and the nose allow the knife to make deep cuts in such a way as to protect the hide. Once the hide is off, cut the skull plate with the horns attached using a saw. Do not use an axe as the impact usually splits the skull plate.

☐ If you wish to enter your trophy into Boone & Crockett or Pope & Younge club, the horns and the skull plate must remain intact. Antlers with split skull plates can be scored but they do not qualify.

CHEAP MAN'S TROPHY

☐ Hunters for the most part like to exhibit their harvest, however, the cost factor comes into play and the next thing you know their is no money in your kitty to get a decent head mount.

When this occurs one can revert to the way of the Swedish head mount. This basically is the skull and antlers of the animals which when tastefully done can look quite impressive.

Bleaching the skull of the animal with the horns attached is a simple process. One can let them bleach naturally by allowing it to bleach in the sun or one can quicken the process as follows.

Skin out the head of your trophy animal removing as much of the meat on it as possible. Remove the eyes and lower jaw. Place about two or three inches of bleach in a metal pail and add sufficient water to cover the skull (not the horns). Bring the water to a boil and add the skull boiling all of the meat off.

After a couple of hours remove any further meat clinging to the skull.

Check the brain cavity to make sure that it is clean. Let the skull dry.

When the skull is dry and bleached white, apply a coat of varnish to it and place it on a plaque on your wall. As an added touch you can paint the skull and make it look like an Indian decoration.

Later on if you wish, you can have the head mounted.

You can do so by using the cape from that animal or from another.

CLEANING YOUR GAME

CHAPTER NINE

CHAPTER NINE
CLEANING GAME ANIMALS

☐ This method can be used for most big game animals. The hunt is over once the animal is down and now the work begins. When you approach a downed animal, do so with caution. It may be still alive and unconscious, if this is the case you could be in for one heck of a surprise. Make sure it is down and out. If you are not sure, put another round into it just to be safe.

How your meat will taste will depend on just how well you clean it, so do it right.

The animal should be cleaned as soon as possible and cooled off. Place the moose on its back and spread the legs open. If you are alone this can be done by tying the rear legs apart between two different trees. Turning the antlers of the moose so that they are against the ground can also help. Use a sharp knife and always remember to cut up away from the fur. Running a knife along the hide or cutting down into the hide will dull your knife quickly. Cut deep into the neck as close to the skull as possible to cut the windpipe. Do not do this if you wish to keep the cape for a head mount.

Make a cut from below the breast bone cutting the hide and the muscles that hold the stomach in. Run the knife from that location to the anus along the belly being careful not to cut open the stomach pouch. Make sure that you leave evidence of sex on the animal on one side of the cut. Cut the pelvic bone open with a saw or an axe and using the knife cut around the anus. Pull it out and tie the end of the anus with a piece of string so that the feces does not fall into the meat. Roll the intestines out of the stomach cavity using caution not to cut them open. Cut the cartilage holding the stomach paunch in place. Place your knife, blade up, between the breast bone and cut upwards towards the head splitting it and the hide at the same time.

Separate the rib cage down the middle and place a stick between them to help hold them apart. Now, reach inside the chest cavity and grab the windpipe and gullet.

Pull the windpipe out of the the chest cavity towards the rear end of the animal and the heart and lungs should follow. Cut out the diaphragm muscles and other membranes which are attached to the inside of the chest cavity. By pulling the windpipe out further you should be able to remove the entire internal organs of the moose. Cut away any membranes that you may have missed. The body cavity should be rolled over on it's side to allow the blood to run out. the body cavity should be wiped out with a damp towel to remove any surplus fluids left in the body. Cut the moose in half using a knife and a saw between the second and the third ribs. Remember to cut with the knife and then cut the backbone with a saw or an axe. Take the hind half and cut along the center of the backbone the full length using a saw, thus quartering your hind quarters. Remove the head cutting it as close to the skull as possible so as not to ruin any neck roasts.

With the head removed, cut the front half into two quarters by using the same method that you used for the hind quarters. Your moose is now quartered. Remove the feet, keeping the tendons intact, and cut a hand hold sized hole at the bottom of the leg between the tendons and the leg bone. In the hind quarters cut another hand hold sized hole along the rib section between the second and the third ribs. In this way you can throw the hind quarter on your back to pack out and have a hand hold on the leg and the rib section. In the front quarters you can do the same except that the hand hold in the rib section can be in a position that is most comfortable to you.

Hang your quarters on a game pole that is high enough that the varmints cannot get to it. Remove the hide. Now rub the meat down with a water and vinegar solution and pick out any dirt or hair that may be on the meat. Wrap the quarters with a cheese cloth or burlap bag to keep the flies and dirt off. When picking a location to hang the meat choose a spot that is not exposed to the sun and is shaded and cool. When transporting the meat ensure that it is in an area that has adequate ventilation and that there are no substances around that can taint the meat such as gas, oil and what have you.

CLEANING YOUR RABBIT

☐ Cleaning a rabbit is very easy, requires little effort and can be done without a knife. It is best to remove the hide as soon as possible after harvesting the little critter as the hide will come off easier. Take the rabbit and hold it securely in one hand near the front shoulders. Place the other hand on the base of the rabbits head and the neck. Twist the head around until the head comes off. Now grab the rabbit with both hands on the fur in the center of the rabbits back. Pull the fur in your right hand towards the rabbits front and at the same time pull the fur in your left hand towards its rear. The skin will easily come off in the direction that you are pulling. Continue to pull until the fur is completely off. You will notice that there are little mittens of fur left on the front and rear paws. Break the rabbits feet and twist them off. Hold the rabbit with one hand, stomach side up, and puncture the stomach skin with a stick or a knife. With this done, force the stomach cavity and remove the contents by pulling them out. Place your hand further into the chest cavity and remove the heart and lungs. Keep the heart as it makes good eating. Cut the rabbit behind the back ribs and you have now halved your rabbit. Now, cut the rabbit across the back in front of the hind legs. This will give you a four to five inch section of meat connected to the back bone. Split the hind quarters down the center of the back. Lift the front legs up away from the rib cage and cut the front legs off. This will give you six portions of the rabbit for your cooking pot. Two hinds, back, two fronts and the rib section as well as the heart. Clean the sections off and let it soak in salt water overnight. This makes a great fried rabbit or stew. This method can also be used on ground squirrels and ground hogs.

CLEANING YOUR DUCKY

There are basically two simple methods to clean your ducks.

The first is to skin them out. Although easy and effective your ducks when cooked will be very dry.

If you wish to have a moister eating bird why not try this method?

Boil three bars of paraffin wax in a metal pail which is half filled with water. As the water heats up it will melt the wax which is floating in the pail and float to the top in liquid form. Pluck your duck, removing as many feathers as possible as well as the wings and head. Keep the feet on. Dip the duck into the pail, holding it by the feet, and submerge it until the entire bird is covered. The wax will surround the entire bird and cling to it when the bird is removed. Hang the bird by the feet using a clothes pin and let the wax harden. Once the wax has hardened and completely cooled take the bird and place it over the pail of melted wax. Remove the wax and allow it to fall back into the pail for reuse. The small pin feathers will come off with the wax leaving only your unskinned bird. Gut the duck, taking out the stomach contents and wash out the body cavity. Cut off the feet and your duck is ready to cook.

☐ Want to find out the live weight of your deer? Divide the dressed weight of the deer by .78612 and you will get his live weight.

WILD
AND
CRAZY
RECIPES

CHAPTER TEN

CHAPTER TEN
WILD AND CRAZY RECIPES

☐ This recipe works great on anything from a buffalo to a goat. To remove the tongue, cut from the center of the bottom lip straight down to the throat. Peel back the skin with your knife outwards and up the sides of the lower jaw. Place your knife inside the lower jaw bone on one side and carefully cut that side the full inside length of the jaw bone cutting any muscles that are holding the tongue. Now do the same thing to the other side of the inside jaw. Reach up inside the bottom of the lower jaw bone, grab the tongue and pull down hard. This will pull the tongue out and down but it will still be attached at the root by muscles and things of the sort. Cut the tongue at the base as far in as possible with your knife. Wash the tongue well in cold water.

Place the tongue in a pot of water and boil it. Add a few pieces of garlic and a sliced onion. The outside skin will start to bubble. Take the tongue out and peel the outside skin off of it. The job will be made easier as the bubbles help the skin come off.
Let the tongue cool and slice it into 1/2 inch sections crossways. Smaller tongues can remain intact.

Make a pickling sauce by getting a jar of a suitable size to hold the tongue. Cut up one onion and place about half of it in the bottom of the jar. Cut up several cloves of garlic and place half of it into the jar as well. Place the sliced tongue in the jar and then add the rest of the garlic and onions. Place about a tablespoon of pickling spices in the jar and add the rest of the tongue. With these ingredients in the jar add white vinegar until the jar is about 3/4 full and fill the rest with cold water. Place a light coating of crushed chilies on top of the solution. If you like a challenge and like it hot add a few shots of Tabasco sauce. Seal the top of the jar and place it in the fridge for at least one week before eating. This recipe also works well with heart.

COUGAR OR LYNX BALLS

Members of the cat family make excellent eating and one should not let it go to waste. It has been said many times that these felines taste a lot like chicken. You be the judge. Cook the meat in large chunks, as you would a roast, using whatever spices meets your culinary pleasure. Once cooked, the meat can be served as the main dish or you can take it one step further and make up your balls. To do this, let the meat cool for several hours and cut it up into one inch squares.

Make a batter using the following
as you lightly mix it together.
2 cups of cold water,
2 eggs, 1/2 teaspoon of baking
soda and 1/2 teaspoon of salt.
Add two cups of unsifted cake
flour. Mix it until the mixture
is blended (this batter will be lumpy). Sprinkle another 2/3 cup of unsifted flour on top of it and with a fork stir up the batter for one or two strokes. Take the pieces of meat and dip them in batter making sure that it covers all of the meat. Remove them and drop them in a deep fryer until they turn brown. Buy some plum, pineapple or cherry sauce and spread it on the balls. Served with a rice dish this makes an excellent meal.

MOOSE NOSE

☐ Remove the fleshy bulbous portion
of the nose from the moose head and
singe all of the hair off of it near an
open fire. Once that is done scrape the

meat clean of the hide and hair that is remaining. Wash the meat well and boil it for about two hours with onions, garlic and seasoning salt. Let it cool and slice it into sections. Sprinkle salt on it if desired and it goes well with beer.

ROAST BEAVER

☐ As beaver is considered a fur bearing animal, it is illegal to hunt them so they must be trapped. The trappers use the beaver meat as bait in their traps. Getting fresh beaver meat from the trapper is just about the most legal way of obtaining it.

When you receive the carcass from the trapper make sure that it is well cleaned out. Wash the meat in cold water and remove any dirt or fur that may have accumulated on it. Boil the beaver in salt water and you will notice that there is a light layer of grease accumulating on the top of the water. This grease or oil comes from the beaver meat. Pour out the water and remove the beaver. Place the beaver carcass in a roast pan and cover it with butter. Smother it in onions, garlic, salt and pepper. Place it in about 1/2 cup of water in the roast pan and cook at 325 degrees fahrenheit until done. This goes great with mashed potatoes and vegetables.

PREPARING BEAVER TAIL

☐ Remove the skin off of the tail by placing it over a campfire's open flame or propane torch. The skin will raise in blisters which you can easily peel off. Once the black skin is removed wash the tail down well. Slice down each side of the tail and throw the bone away. Cut the remaining meat pieces into 1 1/2 inch squares and they are ready for cooking.

BEAVER TAIL AND BEANS

☐ Place the beaver tail in a pot with 1 1/2 cups of navy beans that have been soaked overnight:
1 - chopped onion   3/4 - cup tomato ketchup
1 - tsp salt   1/4 tsp pepper
1 - tbsp brown sugar.
Cover with water and cook until tender.

POTTED TAIL? TAIL CHEESE?

Boil a beaver tail along with a handful of mixed pickling spices tied up in a cheese cloth, salt & pepper. When cooked and boiled down, throw away the spice bag, and turn the remainder into a bread pan and another mold. When cold, this may be sliced for sandwiches.

BAGGED GOOSE.

Roasting goose in a brown paper bag saves cleaning up the oven. Several holes in the bottom of the bag allows the grease to drain out, the bird browns nicely without basting.

SURPRISED MUSKRAT

Muskrats have a yellowish gland behind their front shoulder blades. Take special care to remove that gland prior to cooking as the gland could taint the taste of the meat. Quarter the muskrat in the same manner as you would a rabbit. Take a deep frying pan, add 1 cup of water and place the muskrat in it. Cover the meat with butter and season it. Add a sliced onion, sliced green pepper and garlic cloves. Cover the pan and let it simmer stirring it occasionally until the meat is well done.

What makes this a surprised muskrat? Well, he wasn't expecting to be the main course for dinner.

EATING CROW

□ Contrary to popular belief crows are good to eat. However it is best not to eat crows that are hanging around a dump. Those birds sometimes have a distinct taste to them. Wash the bird off and place a sliced onion in the cavity along with a few pieces of garlic slices. Butter the bird liberally and wrap the crow with slices of bacon. Season the whole thing with seasoning salt, a few onions and some garlic salt. Roll the bird in several folds of tin foil and place it in the oven till the bird is done. Usually one crow with a side order of veggies will feed one person.

EATING BEAR

□ A person once asked me if I have ever eaten bear! I told him no, but I ate in my shorts once.
Actually bear meat is very good. It is a strong dark meat and usually stringy. Slice the meat into thin steak like slices. Fry the meat at a simmer in butter until it is well done. Do not eat rare or medium cooked bear meat. Fry

onions and fresh mushrooms with the meat and add gravy. Allow the mixture to simmer until it gets thick. Serve with mashed potatoes.

BEAR TENDERLOIN

☐ 2-3 pounds of bear tenderloin
To make the sauce: 3/4 cup vinegar, 3/4 cup ketchup, 1 cup water, 1 chopped onion, 1 minced garlic clove, 2 tsp salt, 1/4 tsp pepper, 1 tbsp Worchester sauce, 1/4 tsp Tabasco, 3 tbsp brown sugar, 1 tsp dry mustard. Slice the meat into 1/2 inch slices and cook it in the oven at 350 degrees Fahrenheit. At the same time mix the sauce ingredients together and cook at a medium heat for a half an hour. Cover the meat with the sauce and cook together for one hour.

GROUND HOG DELIGHT

☐ Skin out the ground hog and gut it, clean up the meat with warm water. Cut the animal in the same manner as

you would a rabbit. Slowly boil the
meat in a large pot with onions, salt
and pepper. When the meat is cooked right through, place
it in a frying pan with a light coating of butter to brown it.
Pour the juice from a can of pineapples over it and let it
simmer in the juices before serving.

PORCUPINE FONDUE

One has to be very careful in cleaning a porcupine for,
obvious reasons. The meal however is one to die for. Soak
it in salt water overnight. Remove it and cut your meat
into strips about two inches long and as wide as your
thumb. Roll the strips in a paste comprised of flour,
seasoning salt, pepper and garlic salt. Place it in the
fondue until the meat is cooked.

If you wish to obtain additional copies of the "Hunters Tip Book" or "The Inept Bowhunter"
Please fill out the form below and send it with $12.95 Canadian or $9.95 U.S. per book . Add $1.75 for one book and $2.75 for two or more books for shipping and handling to.

B.S. Publications
P.O. Box 2053
Kelowna, British Columbia
1X 4K5

Name: ....

Address:..

City / Town:..

Province / State: ....Postal /Zip Code: ....

Please check off: Hunters Tip Book (   ) The Inept Bowhunter (   )

Certified check or money order please
U.S. orders must be in U.S. funds

THE INEPT BOWHUNTER

The Inept Bowhunter is a book which is put together from a combination of short stories that have occurred to Bob Marchand as a bowhunter over his many years of attempting to harvest game animals. This humorous yet practical book puts out the stories the way it was seen through the eyes of this bowhunter. In several areas of the book there are some How To's which could be of use to persons who wish to pick up extra hints in pursuit of game. The photos throughout this book are comical and serious. This book is a must read for anyone with a sense of humor and a yearn to learn.